The Invincible.

An Outline of Germanic Philosophy

by

Guido List

Translated by Edred Thorsson
with Illustrations by Timothy Weinmeister
Inspired by O.E. Czesznko

1996
[Cornelius Vetter, 1898]

Translation Copyright © 1996
by Edred Thorsson
Illustrations Copyright © 1996
by Timothy Weinmeister

All rights reserved. No part of this book, either in part or in whole, may be reproduced, transmitted or utilized in any form or by any means electronic, photographic or mechanical, including photocopying, recording, or by any information storage and retrieval system, without the permission in writing from the Publisher, except for brief quotations embodied in literary articles and reviews.

For permissions, or for the serialization, condensation, or for adaptation write the Publisher at the address below.

Published by
LODESTAR
P.O. Box 16
Bastrop, Texas 78602

www.seekthemystery.com

Address

Dear Reader!

hoever reads this book, should read it without prejudice. If what is written in these pages should not agree with your own views, do not let yourself be influenced. "The human will is not the kingdom of heaven." However, if you are struggling for freedom in the light against the dark spirit of materialism, which has already brought so much misery and sickness into the world, then at least don't let yourself be convinced that the human being is only a soulless automaton.

Recognize the divine spark in yourself and look up to the Invincible All-Father.

Foundation

oing their best through the centuries to destroy and wipe out our special (national) characteristics those in power, those who control the education of the people, have pursued the unattainable mirage of a complete equalization of all tribal differences. They have been guided by the unwholesome intention of heading toward the fabrication of a unified type of humanity.

People were blind to the clearly manifest phenomena of the history of the evolution of the human species, people were deaf to the resounding revelations of the divine will in the governance of the forces of Nature; blinded by misguided brotherly love, they proposed an insane doctrine of delusion which promotes a common world community (cosmopolitanism) among all folk-groups with the false conclusion, pregnant with ruination, of having a single flock with a single shepherd.

Only at the beginning of the 19th century did individual thinkers begin to recognize how disastrous those misguided principles and goals function in such an unnatural conditioning of the people, and what dangers they portend in seed-form for the future of all peoples.

The clarion call of these sympathetic thinkers fell like divine sparks of (spirit) into the European family of peoples, which now, led by the best of their contemporaries, flame into a holy fire of unrestricted development individual national characteristics. Out of such a glow of enthusiasm, like the phoenix, the folk will be reborn in its original purity, refined without dross.

Like the dawning of a more beautiful future, the increasingly clearer conviction has shown forth that in the long run no people can be forced to feel, think and to act in ways other than those made possible by the characteristics of their inborn folk-soul; everything that has been forcibly grafted into the folk-soul confuses and dims the essential characteristics of the folk in a more or less short period of time— until self-awareness awakens again and eliminates the foreign elements.

This awakening of the spirit of the folk, this recognition of the foreign and un-nationalistic elements in the basic regulations which have until this point in time governed the science of education push us to look for a nationalistic basis for the education of the folk once again. This is because the salvation of our descendants can only come to flower by means of a well-planned cultivation of a directed development of the character of the folk in a strictly nationalistic sense.

For this reason any education of the folk proceeding in this direction must be founded on a national renaissance, wholesomeness and empowerment. The same is true where centuries of repression have weakened or spoiled this education. It can be once again enforced and established. Wherever it seems to have fallen asleep, it can be awakened to new life. We must work in the direction of steering the national character toward good ends in order to enable the folk to fulfill higher, and even the highest of accomplishments in the future, and at the same time to strive for the goal of reaching the ennobling of the folk all of which is attainable.

But this, the highest goal of the education of the folk, is only attainable when the irrevocable laws of evolution, according to which the All is formed, whereby each advances the development of its own kind and race, are taken into account. But these goals can in no way be attained if a foreign, and often even hostile, spirit is force upon the folk-soul which strives against the thoughts and feelings of that very folk-soul and against the eternal laws of creation and development.

It is therefore above all a compelling necessity to institute a national curriculum for the education of the folk in the schools, and that this is to begin in the earliest grades and continue throughout the schooling to establish such a planned national folk-education by means of a "Folk-Way-Teaching"*[Volkssittenlehre] (National-Morality), which has to be treated as an obligatory educational objective. Therefore this planned national schooling offers the intended fulfillment of the demands of many educators, who are trying to get even the denominational schools to do this, but in place of instruction in religion they want the pupils to be instructed in a comparable moral teaching.

The youth, and therefore the folk of the future, would descend into savagery if the influence of the schools on spiritual and moral education is removed. The "*folk-way-lore" would convey to all pupils of the varied religious denominations, as an obligatory educational objective, a unified, fully developed moral code based on a nationalistic foundation which would ripen into the most beautiful fruit sprouting religiously from a nationalistic sensibility. Such a deep religiosity, which would not germinate from empty belief in formulas but from an innermost living sensibility of the folk-soul, would be the most reliable treasury against the threatening brutalization of the folk and therefore the best defense against the defeat of the nation which would incurably begin with the fading of the folk-ideal.

Just what a salutatory effect such a planned schooling of the spirit would have, especially in Austria, is made clear by the fact that in most of the schools pupils in a given class may consist of Catholics, Protestants – and not seldom old-believers [Alt-Gläubige] – not to mention Jews and Muslims, all of whom are weaned by their specialized religious instruction from the national sensibility and for this reason they are drawn into religious, or better said, denominational, conflicts. If, however, denominational religious education is eliminated from the schools and turned over to private instruction as a private matter, and in its place a folk-moral teaching is instituted as a national morality, which the secular, national teachers would have to present, then the schools could expect to turn out pupils brought up with a sense of nationalism who would be a match for all the coming storms in the state and in everyday life due to the fact that they would have a holy understanding of elevated nationalistic ideas.

With this intimation it is sufficiently emphasized that the nationalist *[folk-moral teaching] is most certainly founded on a religious, note well a religious – and not a denominational – feeling. For awareness of God is particular to each individual but no one will deny the existence of the One, Great and Inscrutable whom our ancestors, from the origin of our folk– that is, long before the rise of Christianity – called God. And this God, whom all "legally recognized religious communities" worship as the father of humanity, and whose laws proclaim the love of homeland and humanity – is always the same in all the main dogmas of all denominations because it is permanently embedded in the heart of every person that this One rules over everything. And so too must the national *[folk-moral teaching] be built upon the recognition of this One God, and his eternal laws, slumbering in the heart of every person, should be awakened and educated for the salvation and blessing of our folk, our fatherland and the future of both.

The present book should also take us a step further, although it is founded on an awareness of God, it is not only the belief, but also the knowledge of the reader which is to be challenged and advanced. None of the precepts offered here contradicts the current state of knowledge in the natural sciences, and so too should the peace between religion and science be initiated– the lack of which has, until today, been the greatest enemy of "faith."

So then the reader finds in the present book a kind of "Short Catechism" which is composed with conscientious attention to all the results of modern scientific investigation, which in no way contradicts worldly wisdom with the results derived from these scientific truths, nor is it incompatible with the views of duty and morality innate in our folk. Herein, in short easy to understand sentences, is expressed a worldview in the Germanic sense of the word. It is a mirror image of the German folk-soul as it is and as it ought to be.

In the view of the author the right way is being shown in this present book which outlines a national doctrine for the morality of the folk— how a noble German folk, healthy in both spirit and body, can be developed— a folk which will be able to withstand all of the storms of the future and which will have to meet the most difficult demands of the times to come .

The Author

An Outline for a Germanic Worldview

In the Form of a Short Catechism

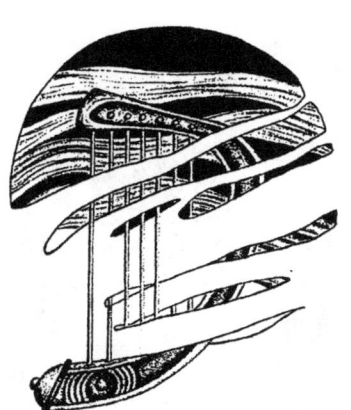

First Chapter

On Knowledge of God

1. What is God?

God is the almighty eternal spirit of the cosmos, the primordial source of life, the paragon of the good, noble and beautiful.

God is the eternal primordial law, the highest will, which rules over all, nothing can come into being or pass away without the will of God.

God is therefore the creator of All and the father of humanity and for this reason we call God "All-Father."

God loves all of his creations, he warns us by means of an inner voice concerning misfortune and danger and always reminds us to do the Good.

God is present everywhere; he knows everything and sees everything and for this reason also knows our most secret thoughts.

He rewards good and punishes evil.

God is most merciful; he forgives us our shortcomings, if we better ourselves.

God is eternal; he was, is, and will always be.

2. In what do we recognize the existence of God, which we cannot see?

Our inner consciousness (the inner voice, conscience, which we call our soul) allows us to perceive and sense the existence of God.

We recognize the existence of God in the voice of Nature, in all that is good, beautiful and noble, which surrounds us, and in the actions of good and noble human beings.

People who close themselves to the recognition of God lose their good cheer, their pure full lust for life, the joy of existence— for God is the primordial source of all life. Quite often such unfortunate children of God take wrong paths, deviate from the way of virtue, and become mean and corrupt.

Second Chapter

On the Creation of the World

1. How did the World Come into Being?

In the beginning it was dark and cold in eternal cosmic space. A cloud – the eternal primeval material – hovered therein. The elements had not yet been differentiated, and the forces of Nature slumbered.

Then God wanted the world to come into being, and he breathed his vivifying breath into the cloud.

The forces of nature awoke, it began to fume and thunder in the yawning primeval material. Bolts of lightning flashed through cosmic space and "There was Light!"

There arose an enormous sea of fire which surged and heaved wildly back and forth until it began to shift and spin like a wheel of fire, sparks and flames of tremendous size working around within it.

From the giant cloud of fire God formed the Sun, and from the flames surrounding it the Earth, the Moon and the Stars. The heavenly bodies which arose in this way all received their set courses according to which we reckon our time. Not everything was like it is now. Our Earth was likewise a fiery, then glowing sphere, which needed uncounted millennia for the surface to cool enough so that a firm crust could form. Through the power of the fire which ruled from within this outermost crust was frequently split apart and the tremendous amounts of rubble caused to tower up toward the heavens; and in this way the mountains came into being. It was, however, to be another untold thousands of years until the Earth had cooled down enough for the cooperation of heat and cold to be able to cause water vapors to precipitate and thereby were formed clouds, springs, [Gäche], rivers, seas and oceans. As air, water and earth were now manifest, God first created plants in the water and on dry land and then fish in the water, birds in the air and animals on dry land.

After the plants and animals had come to life, God finally created man.

2. Why did God Create Man?

God created man that man might recognize and love God, serve him and be contented.

3. How Do We Recognize, Honor, Love and Serve God?

We recognize God in everything good, noble and beautiful that surrounds us.

We recognize God in the governance of the grand and wondrous laws of Nature, and in the works and deeds of good, noble and gifted people.

We should always strive to become better, because this leads to the good and to knowledge of God.

People honor God by completing good, noble and beautiful deeds and actions.

We love God when we give thanks for all that is good, when we attend to the care of our fellow man who is in need, and when we patiently bear the hardships of life.

We serve God when we lead an honest life, practice virtue and conscientiously fulfill our duties.

We serve God when we comfort the unfortunate and help to right injustices.

We serve God when we further the progress of the evolution of his works, when we take part in the ennobling of our folk and make provision for its prosperity and welfare in future times with forethought today.

We serve God when we defend our folk and fatherland in any dangerous situation against inner as well as foreign enemies.

4. How Did God Create Man?

God created us in several kinds of branches, or tribes, from which the various peoples arose-- just as he had caused plants and animals to come into being in many different kinds from the beginning of time.

5. What is a Folk?

Each greater unity of humans, which has its own language, writing system and history, unique in its sense, customs and way of thinking, is called a Folk.

6. Why Did God Cause the Various Folk-groups to Come into Being?

In order to maintain Life.

7. What Is Life?

Life is struggle and the prize of the struggle is Life.

If people could enjoy life without struggle, without work, without all the trials and tribulations life brings with it, then everyone -- given that enough food were available -- would have to grow sick and die due to pure laziness.

It is determined in God's all-wise counsel that all the joys of this life must be won by means of hard work and labor, and that that which has been won should be defended with manly courage.

God loves and protects hard-working, courageous, loyal nations which keep the Right holy, and rewards them with prosperity and freedom. As a reward he sends them great men, who lead them to power, greatness and abundance.

We should respect and appreciate such men, gifted by God, be they heroes, scholars or artists, for God is making use of them as tools to refine, to teach and to delight mankind.

Great men are not measured with the yardstick of the conventional, we must forgive them their short-comings and weaknesses, which even they too have, and must not seek to darken their glorious deeds maliciously.

God turns away from lazy, cowardly, envious and self-serving peoples and punishes them with slavery and destruction.

8. What Do Language and Script Mean?

Language and writing are the highest possessions of mankind; they provide man with that dignity, which separates him from all the other creations in the world.

Through that which has been orally recounted by the tribal elders to their children and to their children's children, we have knowledge of the events of bygone times, which serve as warnings and guidance in the future. The folk-tales and sagas from old, dim prehistory, which are holy to every people, are maintained by means of the mother tongue.

Language and script are likewise the link between God and man. Through language and writing the spirit of long-dead, noble and God-gifted people lives on in us, and we, as well as our most distance descendants, will gain from their merits.

Language is therefore the word of God which has made us into human beings, and writing is holy to us because it reveals the will of God.

9. How Should We Live?

Man should, as a being gifted with reason, be noble and good, do nothing and neglect nothing that stands in contradiction to his own conscience.

We should, when we come to the use of our reason, learn to recognize:

1. That we must earn our livelihoods by hard work and labor, honestly and uprightly.
2. That idleness is a great vice.
3. That the aim of our existence is to live in such a way as to acquire the love and respect of our fellow man.

10. How Do We Acquire the Love and Respect of Our Fellow Man?

We must always hold only good and noble examples before our eyes, strive to refine and ennoble ourselves according to them, and learn to differentiate between good and evil.

11. How Do We Know What is Good and Evil?

1. We recognize what is good and what is evil through our own inner sense, which God place in our hearts and which we call our conscience.
2. We also recognize good and evil by experience. This sense says to good people: "What you don't want, which someone might do to you, that is what you should not do to others."

Experience teaches us that all deeds and actions which preserve that life which has been given to us by God promote the well-being of our family and folk-fellows, and are useful and good; conversely, that such deeds and actions which harm or even destroy our own health, undermine and damage the general welfare of our folk are bad— and therefore evil.

Third Chapter

On the Divine Laws

1. What Things are Called Divine Laws?

Those eternal primordial laws, which All-Father, immutable of all times, has himself marked out in Nature, and which, consciously or unconsciously, all people must follow, to maintain themselves and their kind, are called Divine Laws:

2. What Are these Laws?

1. Acknowledge God and do not disturb others in their faith in God.
2. Fulfill your duties and live in such a way that you gain the love and respect of your fellow man.
3. Maintain the established days of rest and attend divine services with proper devotions on these days.
4. Honor your father and mother and be thankful for the love and care they have given you, happiness and blessedness will then accompany you on the pathways of your life.
5. Preserve your human dignity and do not lower yourself to the level of the predatory beast.
6. Do not lead a degraded life and don't give others a bad example.
7. Do not steal and do not envy others their possessions and property.
8. Observe the law and contracts, do not swear falsely and do not bear false witness.
9. Honor and protect women, keep the family sacred and protect it from hardship and danger.
10. Be true to your folk and fatherland unto death.

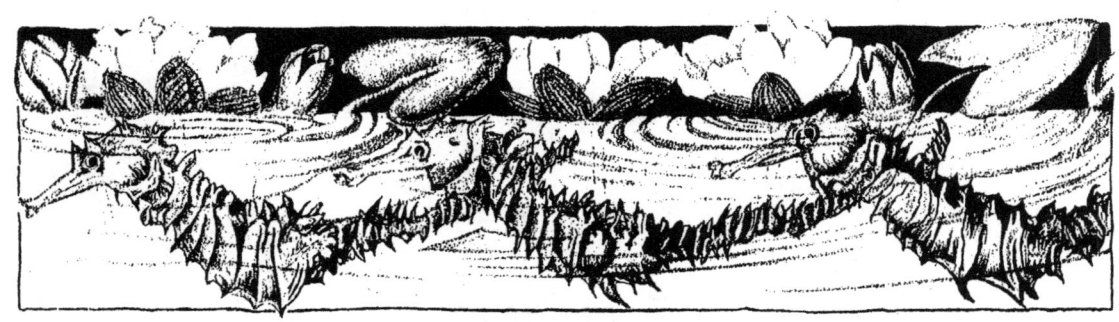

Fourth Chapter

Laws of Custom and Welfare

1. What Are the Laws of Custom and Welfare?
Laws of custom and welfare are those rules of life derived from the divine laws, which are necessary to the upholding of the customary, as well as social life.

2. What Are these Laws?
1. Serve God in your heart and in your deeds, repay good deeds which you have benefited from, encourage good people by your help, punish or prevent injustice.
2. Regret your mistakes and seek to better yourself. Do not enter the House of God when you feel burdened by guilt or unrepentant.
3. Don't be arrogant when fortunate nor despondent when unfortunate.
4. Keep your honor holy and do not degrade yourself; always be just and kind toward others.

3. What Are Transgressions Against these Laws Called?

Every transgression against these laws is called a sin and the greatest sins are those which attract the contempt of our fellow man.

4. What Are the Characteristics, Actions which Are Designated as Sins?

Those characteristics, actions and deeds to be despised as sins are:

1. Arrogance and pride
2. Avarice and greed
3. Insolence and immorality
4. Envy, jealousy, joy in destruction and cruelty
5. Immoderation in food and drink
6. Laziness and idleness
7. Anger and quarrelsomeness

Fifth Chapter

On Virtues and Duties

1. What Are Virtues and Duties?

Duties are those actions which entirely and completely correspond to the divine laws as well as the customs and laws of general welfare, and which everyone is duty-bound to perform. Virtues are the higher ennobling of the duties, upon which the more or less perfect exercise of the degree of love and respect shown to us by our fellow man is dependent.

2. What Are the Main Virtues?

The main virtues are: loyalty, fairness and willingness to sacrifice.

In these high-holy three is concealed the entire requisite of all characteristics of a genuine human being ensouled with a divine spirit— it leads to friendship, love and freedom.

3. How Is this to Be Achieved?

The following rules of life are to be observed to lead a righteous life, respected by all good people, and to be seen as an honorable, upstanding person:

Don't thrust yourself forward with vain egotism, don't try to become conspicuous with empty appearances, and always maintain decorum and good manners.

Your value is to be determined by your fellow man, perhaps even in times to come, never by you yourself.

Your fellow man will soon recognize your worthiness— but then don't be shy, for false modesty is cowardice.

You must repay the love, loyalty and willingness to make sacrifices of other people with your best efforts as well as you can.

Protect the weak and defenseless and don't allow injustice to be committed on them, otherwise you make yourself into an accomplice.

According to the degree to which you follow these rules of life you will soon become a favorite of your fellow man, win good and true friends, and be honored, loved and respected.

And if you meet with malice and ingratitude along your pathway of life, fight courageously and strive to defeat your opponents— but avoid using any dishonest means that would harm you. Consider that life is a struggle and the battle-prize is life itself, but because life is from God and therefore good, the Good must and will be victorious in the end, and so will you if you are righteous.

And even in the most difficult times of struggle you will not be unhappy for:

> "The fulfillment of virtue and duty grants you an elevated consciousness, a blesséd sense of self and a pure conscience, and <u>this is heaven in the heart of man, this sense of happiness is the reward of God</u>."

We wish happiness, blessings and a long life to all doers of good and to their descendants.

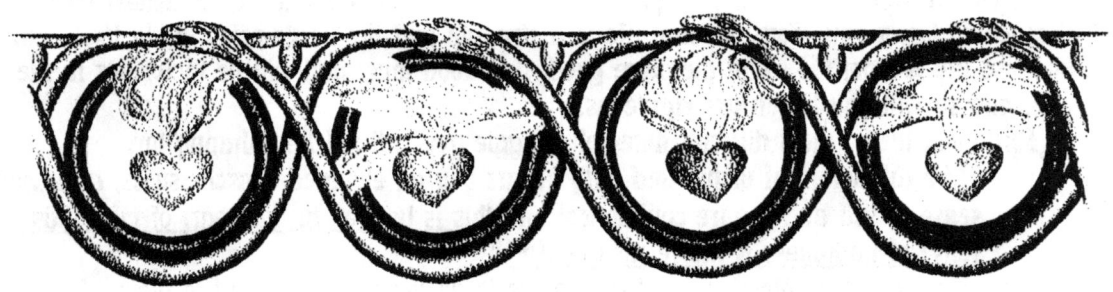

Sixth Chapter

On Vice and Crime

1. What Traits, Actions and Deeds are Characterized as Vices and Crimes?
Just as in Nature where light is opposed to darkness, warmth to cold, life to death, so too is virtue opposed to vice, and duty to crime.

2. What Are the Main Vices?
The greatest vices are: disloyalty and injustice, lying and deception, laziness and base selfishness.

3. What Are Crimes?
All those deeds and actions which in a gross way breech to divine laws, as well as those of customary moral and general welfare, are crimes.

Further, all those deeds and actions which can lead us, our fellow man, our physical descendants or the future of the general folk to deformity, degeneracy or destruction, be that in a physical or spiritual context and thereby can undermine the fortunes of incalculable spans of time in the lives of individuals or of the whole of the folk.

4. How Are Vices and Crimes Recognizable?

Those who, contrary to the will of God, exercise no virtues, perform no duties, and only want to enjoy that which others have acquired and created, are noxious individuals—degenerate, mean and corrupt people.

Their commissions and omissions draw the contempt of the fellow man. They end their lives, abandoned by God, usually before their time or in sickness.

Woe, if they have descendants, for those will be cursed by the avenging conscience of their progenitors.

No one should let themselves be deceived by outer appearances behind which vice seeks to hide itself. That tortuous awareness of guilt – <u>Hell on Earth</u> – is borne in the heart of every base person. Shunned and despised by his fellow man, accursed, the wicked end their miserable existences.

<u>And that is God's punishment!</u>

5. Is Punishment Necessary?

Experience teaches us that malicious people are only roused to greater and greater misdeeds by lenient toleration and indulgence and therefore punishment is necessary.

The severity of the punishment should fit the crime, but it should not be cruel.

Whoever has shown himself unworthy of human company, he shall be imprisoned.

Whosoever has acted as a predator upon his fellow man, he shall be destroyed.

6. Why Is Punishment Necessary?

If the gardener did not clear out the weeds, the hunter did not exterminate the predators, then soon the useful plants would be destroyed and the useful game would be gobbled up.

Seventh Chapter

On Prayer

1. What Is the Purpose of Prayer?
Prayer is an elevation of the spirit to God.

2. How Should We Pray?
We should turn ourselves toward God, our All-Father, with true devotion and heart-felt piety, to thank him for all the good things we have received and ask him for his protection and assistance in a trusting and yielding manner.

We should ask God to give us the power and perseverance to perform our duties and practice our virtues.

We should ask God to give us the power and strength to learn to bear the misfortunes life brings with steadfastness and patience.

We should ask God to help us and stand by us in our hour of need and peril so that we don't give up or fall into doubt.

We should ask God to protect our folk and fatherland from discord and conflict and to provide us with peace, power and freedom through "unity."

Eighth Chapter

On Dying and Death

1. Do We Humans Have to Die, and What Is Death?

According to God's all-wise decree it was determined that nothing could remain as it is for an eternal time, but rather that everything in the world should continuously change and finally return to the primeval condition out of which it evolved— and this return is what we call dying.

Since man too, like everything on Earth, rose from the eternal prima materia, so too must the body return thither when it becomes old or unsuited to life.

Our soul, the park of God, which dwells within us, will be reunified with God and our bodies will return to Mother Earth who gave us birth.

Whether reward or punishment awaits us after death— that God alone knows. Humans shouldn't ponder things knowledge of which God, in his omniscience, has hidden from us.

God may allow the immortal souls of good, noble and meritorious persons live on after their deaths in their children, descendants and folk-fellows as blessed protective spirits.

We ought to remember their working in our lives with thanks in sanctified moments of meditation, and their blesséd deeds should be illuminating models for us.

And because we can not live forever and irrevocable fate has determined that forever and ever age is to be rejuvenated by death, we will bear the inevitable with dignity and forbearance.

God, the All-Father, would not have put anything upon his children if it had not been inexorably required by necessity and impossible to avoid.

Therefore, in divine trust and good conscience we await the hour in which All-Father calls us back to him.

Ninth Chapter

On the End of the World

1. Are Only Humans, Animals and Plants Subject to Death?

Everything that is born in the wide world of God dies again, regardless of whether its existence is for hours, days, years or countless aeons; beginning and end is allotted to all, only God alone is without beginning and end.

2. Will Our Earth also Come to an End or Die?

Our great Earth, upon which we live, also is subject to this primeval law of God. But we can take as our consolation that the life-span of our Mother Earth is much too great to put us in a position to be able to perceive a diminishing of the life-force of the Earth any more than a one-day fly could conceive of our human life-span. This is due to the relatively meaningless brevity of our lives, and to the short span of time which comprises human history.

3. How Will the Death of the Earth Be Prepared for and How Will it Come about?

The sun will not eternally appear the way it now shines and warms things. A time will come when it will only glow red until it finally goes out completely. But long before the extinguishing of the Sun the vivifying springs of our Earth will have run dry and our beautiful rivers and lakes, our broad oceans will have dried up. There will be no more air and no more clouds, not even plants and animals. It will be desolate and empty on the Earth, as it is upon the Moon, where this condition has already come about today.

It will be once more dark and cold, and everything, which will arise, will fragment in the monstrous cold and dissolve into the eternal primeval matter.

*A star is extinguished, another will begin to shine—
thus it is written in the Book of Nature. —*

The End

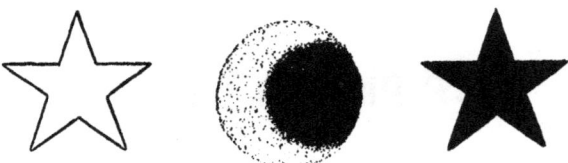

Appendix

A Historical Note on *The Invincible*

The following passage was written by Johannes Balzili in his 1917 biography of Guido von List:

... *The Invincible, an Outline of Germanic Philosophy* appeared in 1898. *The Invincible* is a kind of catechism. The story of the origin of this little book is worth recounting. In the summer of 1898 the state government of Lower Austria passed a law that mandated religious instruction for middle-school (gymnasium) pupils. The cardinal and Arch-Bishop of Vienna (Dr. Gruschen) spoke up for the law as did the state marshall Prince Alois Liechtenstein and the eventual mayor of Vienna, Dr. Karl Lueger. Subsequently in a council of voters of the 6th district of Vienna representative K. H. Wolf requested an official opinion from Dr. Lueger concerning the law. Dr. Lueger answered "Give us something better and we will follow you!" Guido von List was deeply effected by all this. Overnight, that is from one day to the next, he wrote down his catechism "The Invincible," without sleeping, on the next day he went to visit representative Wolf and delivered the finished manuscript to him with the words: "So, there you have something better!" But Wolf rejected the idea right away, because for him "Religion was only an academic thing." Even if nothing was to be gained in this way— "The Invincible" was nevertheless printed and soon 5000 copies had been sold. Even if today "The Invincible" is, as the Master himself says, "antiquated," because it has been "superseded by much deeper knowledge," nevertheless back then it was a beginning. *The Invincible* is therefore in a certain sense a historical marker, and it was no exaggeration when during a conversation in the Master's apartment on the 6th of January 1898 the old Catholic bishop Nittel von Warnsdorf in German Bohemia said that from Guido von List's desk "a new epoch in the history of religion will go forth!"

The artwork for this volume was created by Timothy Weinmeister, closely based on the art of O.C. Czesznko which accompanied the 1898 edition of *Der Unbesiegbare*. Weinmeister meticulously creates his remarkable works using only ballpoint pens. He is also represents the second generation in his family to study the work of Guido von List.

www.ingramcontent.com/pod-product-compliance
Lightning Source LLC
Chambersburg PA
CBHW081503040426
42446CB00016B/3371